W9-BMK-400

Date: 4/13/11

J 796.323 CZE
Czeskleba, Abby.
Cool basketball facts /

PALM BEACH COUNTY
LIBRARY SYSTEM
3650 SUMMIT BLVD.
WEST PALM BEACH, FLORIDA 33406

Pebble® Plus

Cool Sports Facts

Cool Basketball Facts

by Abby Czeskleba

Consulting Editor: Gail Saunders-Smith, PhD

Consultant: Craig Coenen, PhD
Associate Professor of History
Mercer County Community College
West Windsor, New Jersey

CAPSTONE PRESS
a capstone imprint

Pebble Plus is published by Capstone Press,
151 Good Counsel Drive, P.O. Box 669, Mankato, Minnesota 56002.
www.capstonepub.com

Copyright © 2011 by Capstone Press, a Capstone imprint. All rights reserved.
No part of this publication may be reproduced in whole or in part, or stored in a retrieval system, or transmitted in any
form or by any means, electronic, mechanical, photocopying, recording, or otherwise, without written permission of the
publisher. For information regarding permission, write to Capstone Press,
151 Good Counsel Drive, P.O. Box 669, Dept. R, Mankato, Minnesota 56002.

Books published by Capstone Press are manufactured with paper
containing at least 10 percent post-consumer waste.

Library of Congress Cataloging-in-Publication Data
Czeskleba, Abby.
  Cool basketball facts / by Abby Czeskleba.
    p. cm.—(Pebble plus. Cool sports facts)
  Includes bibliographical references and index.
  Summary: "Simple text and full-color photos illustrate facts about the rules, equipment, and records of basketball"—
Provided by publisher.
  ISBN 978-1-4296-4478-5 (library binding)
  1. Basketball—Miscellanea—Juvenile literature. I. Title. II. Series.

GV885.1.C94 2011
796.323—dc22   2009051409

Editorial Credits
Erika L. Shores, editor; Kyle Grenz, designer; Eric Gohl, media researcher; Eric Manske, production specialist

Photo Credits
Comstock Images, cover (basketball), back cover, 1
Dreamstime/Mike Liu, cover
NBAE via Getty Images Inc./David Liam Kyle, 5; Dick Raphael, 7; Jesse D. Garrabrant, 13, 21; Lisa Blumenfeld, 15;
    Melissa Majchrzak, 11; Nathaniel S. Butler, 19; Noah Graham, 17
Newscom/Icon SMI/Albert Pena, 9

Note to Parents and Teachers

The Cool Sports Facts series supports national social studies standards related to people, places, and culture. This book describes and illustrates basketball. The images support early readers in understanding the text. The repetition of words and phrases helps early readers learn new words. This book also introduces early readers to subject-specific vocabulary words, which are defined in the Glossary section. Early readers may need assistance to read some words and to use the Table of Contents, Glossary, Read More, Internet Sites, and Index sections of the book.

Printed in the United States of America in North Mankato, Minnesota.
122010   006032R

Table of Contents

Slam Dunk!

Each year, NBA players
slam dunk in front of
21 million fans.
In 2009, players dunked
more than 9,000 times.

NBA stands for National Basketball Association.

Cool Equipment

In 1985, Michael Jordan wore different shoes than his teammates. He broke NBA rules. The NBA fined him $5,000 for each game.

Michael Jordan

Teams get six basketballs to use during warm-ups before a game. The number of balls is listed in the NBA rule book.

Cool Rules

A team with the basketball

has 24 seconds to take a shot.

A player must shoot

a free throw within

10 seconds.

shot clock

It's against the rules

to kick the ball on purpose.

Kicking the ball into the stands

gets the player kicked out

of the game.

Cool Records

The Women's National
Basketball Association
began in 1997.
Lisa Leslie scored
the first dunk in the WNBA.

In 2008, Jordan Farmar set
a dribbling record.
At the NBA All-Star Jam
Session, Farmar dribbled
a ball 228 times in one minute.

NBA star Robert Parish played

in 1,611 NBA games.

No one has played more

NBA games than he has.

The Boston Celtics have won the most NBA championships with 17. They won 11 of these championships in just 13 years.

Glossary

dribble—to bounce a basketball off the floor using one hand

dunk—when a player jumps above the basketball rim with the basketball and throws it in the net

fine—to charge someone money for breaking a rule

free throw—a shot taken from the free-throw line by a player when the other team makes a foul

Read More

Franks, Katie. *I Want to Be a Basketball Player.* Dream Jobs. New York: PowerKids Press, 2007.

Ladewski, Paul. *Stars on the Court.* New York: Scholastic, 2009.

Internet Sites

FactHound offers a safe, fun way to find Internet sites related to this book. All of the sites on FactHound have been researched by our staff.

Here's all you do:

Visit *www.facthound.com*

FactHound will fetch the best sites for you!

Index

Word Count: 190

Grade: 1

Early-Intervention Level: 21